THE
ROSARY
of SAINT JOHN PAUL II

THE
ROSARY
of SAINT JOHN PAUL II

Meditations, Prayers, and Practical Aids

TOM HOOPES

HOLY HEROES BOOKS · CRAMERTON, NORTH CAROLINA

Nihil Obstat:
Leon Suprenant
Censor Deputatus
Imprimatur:
Most Reverend Joseph F. Naumann
Archbishop of Kansas City in Kansas
22 February 2018

The *Nihil Obstat* and *Imprimatur* are a declaration that a book or pamphlet is considered to be free from doctrinal or moral error. It is not implied that those who have granted the *Nihil Obstat* and *Imprimatur* agree with the contents, opinions or statements expressed.

Text by Tom Hoopes
Cover art by Chris Pelicano. Interior art by RestoredTraditions.com.

Excerpts from the Apostolic Letter, *Rosarium Virginis Mariae* (The Rosary of the Virgin Mary) taken from the Vatican website (w2.vatican.va).

Excerpts from the Revised Standard Version of the Bible, 2nd edition, ©1971 by the Division of Christian Education of the National Council of the Churches of Christ in the United States of America. Used by permission. All rights reserved. Some Scripture texts in this work are taken from the New American Bible, revised edition ©2010, 1991, 1986, 1970 Confraternity of Christian Doctrine, Washington, D.C. and are used by permission of the copyright owner. All Rights Reserved. No part of the New American Bible may be reproduced in any form without permission in writing from the copyright owner.

Excerpts from the English translation of the Catechism of the Catholic Church for use in the United States of America. Copyright ©1994, United States Catholic Conference, Inc.—Libreria Editrice Vaticana. Used with permission.

Printed in the U.S.A. ISBN: 978-1-936330-77-5

CONTENTS

Rediscover the Rosary!

Our family didn't always pray the Rosary every day. Like many others, we started after September 11, 2001, when Pope John Paul II called for daily Rosaries for peace, and kept it up until, a year later, John Paul II gave our daily Rosary a second wind.

It wasn't until the Year of the Rosary that we started to see just how serious Pope John Paul II was about this.

"I look to all of you, brothers and sisters of every state of life—to you, Christian families, to you, the sick and elderly, and to you, young people: Confidently take up the Rosary once again," he wrote in his apostolic letter *Rosarium Virginis Mariae*, "Rediscover the Rosary in the light of Scripture, in harmony with the Liturgy, and in the context of your daily lives. May this appeal of mine not go unheard!" (*Rosarium*, 43).

How could we refuse that last line? We have said at least a decade (usually five) practically every day since.

We have come to realize that we as a family can't afford to skip our daily Rosary … and I am convinced that the world can't afford to have Catholics skip our daily Rosaries, either.

Here are five things daily Rosaries do.

Daily Rosaries transform the world.

Pope John Paul II was hailed for hastening the collapse of the Soviet Union by encouraging freedom in his native Poland.

But he had a different understanding of what happened: he thought the Rosary did it, thanks to the worldwide daily Rosaries inspired by the Fatima apparitions.

"We must be wary of oversimplification," he wrote in *Crossing the Threshold of Hope*, but "what are we to say of the three children from Fatima who suddenly, on the eve of the October Revolution, heard: 'Russia will convert' and 'In the end my Immaculate Heart will triumph'?"

He saw no reason that the same woman who solved the Soviet crisis couldn't solve our world's problems today.

"Today I willingly entrust to the power of this prayer," he proclaimed, "the cause of peace in the world and the cause of the family" (*Rosarium*, 39).

Daily Rosaries transform families.

People think of "the family that prays together stays together" as a quaint old saying. But it was a favorite saying of Saint John Paul II and Saint Teresa of Calcutta, and the daily practice of Pope Benedict XVI's family, according to his brother's biographer. Pope Francis says he keeps two things in his pockets at all times: a Rosary and a *Way of the Cross* booklet.

We have found over the years that when we pray the Rosary, we grow closer and stronger as a family—almost automatically. This goes for partial Rosaries (sometimes we only say one decade, or three decades), hurried Rosaries, bored Rosaries, in-the-car Rosaries, distracted Rosaries, or any Rosary.

Why? Saint John Paul II describes why in his letter on the Rosary: "To pray the Rosary for children, and even more, with children, training them from their earliest years to experience this daily 'pause for prayer' with the family … is a spiritual aid which should not be underestimated"(*Rosarium*, 42).

The Rosary stops a busy family in its tracks, quiets the world's noise, gathers us together, and focuses us on God and not ourselves. This does wonders for a family psychologically and emotionally. But it does far more.

John Paul II asked that Rosaries be said for a "critical contemporary issue: the family, the primary cell of society, increasingly menaced by forces of disintegration on both the ideological and practical planes, so as to make us fear for the future of this fundamental and indispensable institution and, with it, for the future of society as a whole."

"The revival of the Rosary in Christian families," he added, "will be an effective aid to countering the devastating effects of this crisis."

The daily Rosary strengthens us against sin.

We may think we are virtuous or good, but it doesn't take much for an unexpected temptation to defeat us.

"We do not pretend that life is all beauty," John Paul II once said. "We are aware of darkness and sin, of poverty and pain. But we know Jesus has conquered sin and passed through His own pain to the glory of the Resurrection. And we live in the light of His Paschal Mystery—the mystery of His Death and Resurrection."

The Rosary returns us to the light of Christ again and again. We need that.

As the *Catechism of the Catholic Church* (and *Gaudium et Spes*) shockingly puts it: "Man has to struggle to do what is right, and it is at great cost to himself, and aided by God's grace, that he succeeds in achieving his own inner integrity."

Scripture's answer to this problem is the repeated injunction to "watch and pray." If we hope to stand a chance in our Christian life, we need regular, systematic, focused time to reconnect ourselves to the spiritual strength of Jesus Christ, our Lord and Brother, and Mary, our heavenly Mother.

We need to repeat the Lord's Prayer, begging the Father to forgive us and deliver us from temptation. We need to ask Mary to pray for us, sinners.

We need the Rosary.

The daily Rosary can transform your life.

Everyone who met Saint John Paul II or Saint Teresa of Kolkata knew that there was something special about them. They were self-possessed but not aloof, gentle but unwavering in what counts, and looked at each person they met with deep attention and concern.

They didn't have that character because they were naturally wonderful people: it came from prayer. And we, too, can gain a little bit of what they had, if we pray.

"Just as two friends, frequently in each other's company, tend to develop similar habits," John Paul wrote, "so too, by holding familiar converse with Jesus and the Blessed Virgin, by meditating on the mysteries of the Rosary and by living the same life in Holy Communion, we can become, to the extent of our lowliness, similar to them and can learn from these supreme models a life of humility, poverty, hiddenness, patience, and perfection" (*Rosarium*, 15).

The daily Rosary can transform your death.

A family we know tells the story of how devoted the father was to the Rosary. He insisted that his family say the Rosary each night at 6:30 p.m. If guests were visiting, those guests would say the Rosary at 6:30 p.m. with them. If saying the Rosary at

6:30 p.m. would interfere with the start time of a school or sporting event, then the family would be late for that event. The Rosary came first.

In his old age, when their father was dying in the hospital, his adult children came to be with him and their mother. They decided that they should say a Rosary for him at the bedside. As they finished the Rosary, he died. They looked up at the clock. It was 6:30 p.m.

There are many such stories. Mary, it seems, really does look out for us "now and at the hour of our death."

Saint John Paul's apostolic letter ends with these lines:

"You will be our comfort in the hour of death: yours our final kiss as life ebbs away. And the last word from our lips will be your sweet name, O Queen of the Rosary … O dearest Mother, O Refuge of Sinners, O Sovereign Consoler of the Afflicted. May you be everywhere blessed, today and always, on earth and in Heaven" (*Rosarium*, 43).

Saying the Rosary daily deepens our Catholic identity, touches our loved ones, and moves Heaven and earth for our intentions. The saints all recommend daily meditative prayer; the Rosary is exactly that. To have a real relationship with Christ, we need to know Him and talk to Him. The Rosary reveals the major events of His life in prayer.

There really is no good reason *not* to pray the Rosary, daily.

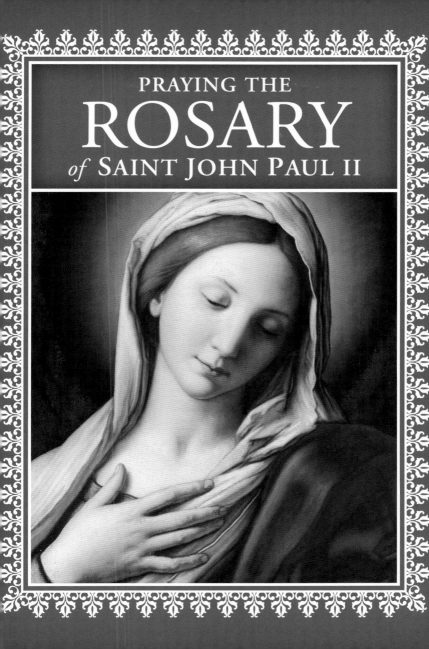

PRAYING THE
ROSARY
of SAINT JOHN PAUL II

The Method of Saint John Paul II

In his October 2002 apostolic letter *Rosarium Virginis Mariae* (The Rosary of the Virgin Mary), Pope John Paul II proposed a new method for this traditional Catholic contemplative prayer to "help the faithful understand [the Rosary] in the richness of its symbolism and in harmony with the demands of daily life … to produce the intended spiritual effects" (*No.* 28).

This book contains the tools, enumerated below and on page 17, to help you apply his method of praying the Rosary and inspire your contemplation of the mysteries of the Faith.

1. As an option to introducing the Rosary with the Creed, say the opening words of Psalm 70: **"O God, come to my aid; O Lord, make haste to help me."** (*No.* 37).

2. Announce each mystery and display a **pictorial representation of the mystery** "*to open up a scenario* on which to focus our attention" (*No.* 29, italics in original).

14

2. Each mystery is accompanied by artwork.

THE JOYFUL MYSTERIES

THE LUMINOUS MYSTERIES

THE SORROWFUL MYSTERIES

THE GLORIOUS MYSTERIES

3. Read a related Biblical passage: "As we listen, we are certain this is the Word of God, spoken for today and spoken 'for me'" (*No. 30*). This booklet provides ten verses per mystery so it can be used as a "scriptural rosary."

4. Observe a short silence after the reading. *(No. 31)*

5. In each Hail, Mary add a clause after saying, "Jesus," as a "*profession of faith* and an aid in concentrating our meditation" (*No. 33*, italics in original).

6. The Glory Be should be given "due prominence" as "*the high point of contemplation*" in the Rosary. In public recitation it could be sung (*No. 34*, italics in original).

7. Conclude each mystery "with a *prayer for the fruits specific to that particular mystery*" that we may "imitate what they contain and obtain what they promise" (*No. 35*, italics in original).

8. Close by praying for the Holy Father's intentions and a prayer in praise of the Blessed Virgin, either the *Salve Regina* or the Litany of Loreto. (*No. 37*).

The Litany of Loreto is on page 106 of this booklet.

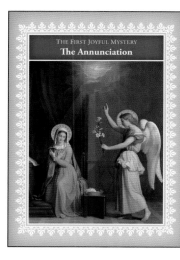

THE FIRST JOYFUL MYSTERY
The Annunciation

**Mary is asked to be
the Mother of Baby Jesus.**

FRUIT OF THE MYSTERY
That I will be quick to follow God's will.

Ten verses from Luke 1:26-38. The angel Gabriel was sent from God to a city of Galilee named Nazareth, | to a virgin betrothed to a man whose name was Joseph. | And he came to her and said, "Hail Mary, full of grace!" | But she was greatly troubled at the saying, and considered in her mind what sort of greeting this might be. | And the angel said to her, "Do not be afraid, Mary, for you have found favor with God. | Behold, you will conceive in your womb and bear a son, and you shall call His name Jesus. | He will be called great, and will be called Son of the Most High." | And Mary said to the angel, "How shall this be, since I have no husband?" | And the angel said, "The Holy Spirit will come upon you, and the power of the Most High will overshadow you; | Therefore the child to be born will be called holy, the Son of God." | And Mary said, "Behold, I am the handmaid of the Lord; let it be to me according to your word."

21

The Annunciation

Ten simple reflections

Mary's Yes

- This mystery is mentioned in the Creed: "He came down from Heaven, and by the Holy Spirit was incarnate of the Virgin Mary, and became man."
- Mary said "yes" in the name of all human nature (*Catechism of the Catholic Church*, 511).
- What Eve lost through disobedience, Mary gained again by obedience (*CCC*, 494).

The Unborn Savior

- This is the moment of the Incarnation, when God becomes man; when "the Word becomes flesh." God becomes a tiny embryo.
- Adam, "the first man, was from earth, a man of the dust; the second Man [Jesus] is from Heaven" (*CCC*, 504).
- God became an embryo—I shouldn't refuse opportunities that would be good even if I think them "beneath me."

22

Add after "Jesus," in each Hail Mary
...and blessed is the fruit of thy womb, Jesus,
conceived in you by the Holy Spirit.

Mary, Our Mother

- Since Christians are the Mystical Body of Christ, Mary became our mother, too, at the Annunciation (*CCC*, 973).
- As He does with Mary, God wants to become intimately and closely associated with me.

Mary, Our Model

- Messengers of God, in daily circumstances and opportunities, come to me, too. I need only pay attention.
- Mary says yes to God without knowing the whole picture— what will happen and how it all will end. I shouldn't demand of God to give me the whole picture, either.

*Pray for me, Mary, cause of our joy,
that I will be quick to follow God's will.*

23

APOSTOLIC LETTER
Rosarium Virginis Mariae

AN EXCERPT ON
THE JOYFUL MYSTERIES

Mysteries to be prayed on Monday and Saturday

(20.) The first five decades, the Joyful Mysteries, are marked by *the joy radiating from the event of the Incarnation*. This is clear from the very first mystery, the Annunciation, where Gabriel's greeting to the Virgin of Nazareth is linked to an invitation to messianic joy: "Rejoice, Mary." The whole of salvation history, in some sense the entire history of the world, has led up to this greeting. If it is the Father's plan to unite all things in Christ (cf. Ephesians 1:10), then the whole of the universe is in some way touched by the divine favor with which the Father looks upon Mary and makes her the Mother of His Son. The whole of humanity, in turn, is embraced by the *fiat* with which she readily agrees to the will of God.

Exultation is the keynote of the encounter with Elizabeth, where the sound of Mary's voice and the presence of Christ in her womb cause John to "leap for joy" (cf. Luke 1:44). Gladness also fills the scene in Bethlehem, when the birth of the divine Child, the Savior of the world, is announced by the song of the angels and proclaimed to the shepherds as "news of great joy" (Lk 2:10).

The final two mysteries, while preserving this climate of joy, already point to the drama yet to come. The Presentation in the Temple not only expresses the joy of the Child's consecration and the ecstasy of the aged Simeon; it also records the prophecy that Christ will be a "sign of contradiction" for Israel and that a sword will pierce His mother's heart (cf. Luke 2:34-35). Joy mixed with drama marks the fifth mystery, the finding of the twelve-year-old Jesus in the Temple. Here He appears in His divine wisdom as He listens and raises questions, already in effect one who "teaches". The revelation of His mystery as the Son wholly dedicated to His Father's affairs proclaims the radical nature of the Gospel, in which even the closest of human relationships are challenged by the absolute demands of the Kingdom. Mary and Joseph, fearful and anxious, "did not understand" His words (Luke 2:50).

To meditate upon the "Joyful" Mysteries, then, is to enter into the ultimate causes and the deepest meaning of Christian joy. It is to focus on the realism of the mystery of the Incarnation and on the obscure foreshadowing of the mystery of the saving Passion. Mary leads us to discover the secret of Christian joy, reminding us that Christianity is, first and foremost, *euangelion*, "good news," which has as its heart and its whole content the person of Jesus Christ, the Word made flesh, the one Savior of the world.

THE FIRST JOYFUL MYSTERY
The Annunciation

Mary is asked to be
the Mother of Jesus.

FRUIT OF THE MYSTERY

That I will be quick to follow God's will.

Ten verses from Luke 1:26-38. The angel Gabriel was sent from God to a city of Galilee named Nazareth, │ to a virgin betrothed to a man whose name was Joseph. │ And he came to her and said, "Hail Mary, full of grace!" │ But she was greatly troubled at the saying, and considered in her mind what sort of greeting this might be. │ And the angel said to her, "Do not be afraid, Mary, for you have found favor with God. │ Behold, you will conceive in your womb and bear a son, and you shall call His name Jesus. He will be called great, and will be called Son of the Most High." │ And Mary said to the angel, "How shall this be, since I have no husband?" │ And the angel said, "The Holy Spirit will come upon you, and the power of the Most High will overshadow you; │ Therefore the child to be born will be called holy, the Son of God." │ And Mary said, "Behold, I am the handmaid of the Lord; let it be to me according to your word."

The Annunciation

Ten simple reflections

Mary's Yes

- This mystery is mentioned in the Creed: "He came down from Heaven, and by the Holy Spirit was incarnate of the Virgin Mary, and became man."

- Mary said "yes" in the name of all human nature (*Catechism of the Catholic Church*, 511).

- What Eve lost through disobedience, Mary gained again by obedience (*CCC*, 494).

The Unborn Savior

- This is the moment of the Incarnation, when God becomes man; when "the Word becomes flesh." God becomes a tiny embryo.

- Adam, "the first man, was from earth, a man of the dust; the second Man [Jesus] is from Heaven" (*CCC*, 504).

- God became an embryo—I shouldn't refuse opportunities that would be good even if I think them "beneath me."

...and blessed is the fruit of thy womb, Jesus,
conceived in you by the Holy Spirit.

Mary, Our Mother

- Since Christians are the Mystical Body of Christ, Mary became our mother, too, at the Annunciation *(CCC, 973)*.
- As He does with Mary, God wants to become intimately and closely associated with me.

Mary, Our Model

- Messengers of God, in daily circumstances and opportunities, come to me, too. I need only pay attention.
- Mary says yes to God without knowing the whole picture— what will happen and how it all will end. I shouldn't demand of God to give me the whole picture, either.

Pray for me, Mary, cause of our joy,
that I will be quick to follow God's will.

Mary visits Elizabeth.

FRUIT OF THE MYSTERY
That I will bring Christ into the lives of others.

Ten verses from Luke 1:36-56. The angel said, "And behold, your kinswoman Elizabeth in her old age has also conceived a son." | Mary arose and went with haste into the hill country, to a city of Judah, and she entered the house of Zechari'ah and greeted Elizabeth. | And when Elizabeth heard the greeting of Mary, the babe leaped in her womb; and Elizabeth was filled with the Holy Spirit | and she exclaimed with a loud cry, "Blessed are you among women, and blessed is the fruit of your womb! | And why is this granted me, that the mother of my Lord should come to me? | For behold, when the voice of your greeting came to my ears, the babe in my womb leaped for joy. | And blessed is she who believed that there would be a fulfillment of what was spoken to her from the Lord." | And Mary said, "My soul magnifies the Lord, | and my spirit rejoices in God my Savior." | And Mary remained with her about three months, and returned to her home.

The Visitation

Ten simple reflections

Honoring Mary

● The angel Gabriel's words, "Hail Mary, full of grace," and Elizabeth's words, "Blessed among women" and "mother of my Lord," together make up the bulk of the Hail Mary prayer.

● Mary is humble but says the Magnificat ("My soul magnifies the Lord . . ."). The humble recognize their giftedness and worth, which come from God.

The Unborn Savior

● Mary left "in haste" to visit Elizabeth, who was a week's journey away.

● John the Baptist's first act of witness to Jesus Christ was to leap in the womb of his mother.

● Christ is the center of these scenes, but He stays hidden, unseen, as He does in our lives.

...and blessed is the fruit of thy womb, Jesus,
whom you carried to Elizabeth.

Mary, Our Mother

- It is Christ in her that makes Mary attractive and that draws people's attention. He wants to use me in the same way.
- Mary is quick to aid Elizabeth; she will be quick to aid me.

Christ in Our Lives

- Like Elizabeth, we should be eager to recognize Jesus in others.
- Like Mary, we should bring Christ into the homes of others.
- Mary's first Christian apostolate was doing household chores. Mostly, our Christian life means small things done with love.

Pray for me, Mary, cause of our joy,
that I will bring Christ into the lives of others.

The Nativity

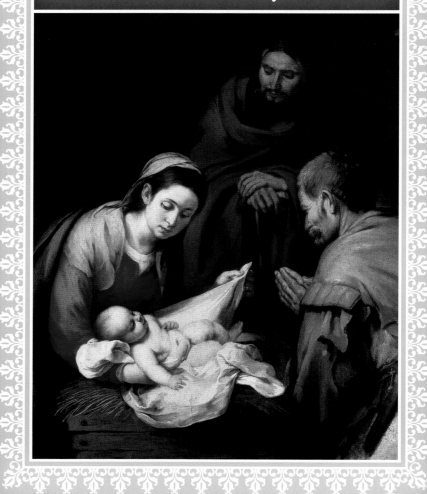

Jesus is born in Bethlehem.

FRUIT OF THE MYSTERY
That I will make Christ the center of my family.

Ten verses from Luke 2:4-20. And Joseph also went up to the city of David, which is called Bethlehem, to be enrolled with Mary, his betrothed. │ And she gave birth to her first-born Son and wrapped Him in swaddling clothes, and laid Him in a manger, │ because there was no place for them in the inn. │ And in that region there were shepherds out in the fields, keeping watch over their flock by night. │ And an angel of the Lord appeared to them, and the glory of the Lord shown around them, and they were filled with fear. │ And the angel said to them, "Be not afraid; for behold, I give you good news of great joy, for to you is born this day in the city of David a Savior, who is Christ the Lord. │ And this will be a sign for you: you will find a Babe wrapped in swaddling clothes and lying in a manger." │ And suddenly there was with the angel a multitude of the heavenly host praising God and saying, "Glory to God in the highest, and on earth peace among men with whom He is pleased." │ And they went with haste, and found Mary and Joseph, and the Babe lying in a manger. │ Mary kept all these things, pondering them in her heart.

The Nativity

Ten simple reflections

The Humble God

- Imagine being all-powerful God and limiting yourself to the abilities of a baby. That's love.

- Shepherds were not known for being religious. But they were the first to receive the Good News. Jesus wants to reach everyone with His message.

- We can count on God's answers to our prayers, but often in unexpected ways—a stable instead of a room.

The Innkeeper

- The world usually either bitterly opposes Christ, like Herod, or is indifferent to Him, like the innkeepers.

- Baby Jesus had no words to offer, only His presence. And that was enough to attract a lot of attention.

- Christ can be quiet, almost imperceptible. He's also the God of glory, angel choirs, and giant stars.

- An innkeeper who could have been transformed by Jesus— even his business might have prospered—refused. How often do we refuse to let Christ into our lives?

...and blessed is the fruit of thy womb, Jesus,
born in Bethlehem.

The Wise Men

- "The Magi's coming to Jerusalem in order to pay homage to the King of the Jews shows that they seek in Israel the . . . King of the nations" (*CCC*, 528).
- The Wise Men read the books, learned where to find Christ, and traveled for days to meet Him. For us He is in our own Catholic church, in the tabernacle.
- The Wise Men give their best to God. Do we give our best time, best efforts, best talents?

Pray for me, Mary, cause of our joy,
that I will make Christ the center of my family.

The Presentation

Mary and Joseph present
Jesus in the Temple.

FRUIT OF THE MYSTERY

That I will always be ready to encounter Christ.

Ten verses from Luke 2:22-40. They brought Him up to Jerusalem to present Him to the Lord | and to offer a sacrifice according to what is said in the law of the Lord, "a pair of turtledoves, or two young pigeons." | Now there was a man in Jerusalem, whose name was Simeon, and this man was righteous and devout. | And it had been revealed to him by the Holy Spirit that he should not see death before he had seen the Lord's Christ. | When the parents brought in the Child Jesus . . . he took Him up in his arms and blessed God. | And he said, "Lord, now lettest thou thy servant depart in peace, according to Thy word; | for mine eyes have seen Thy salvation which Thou hast prepared in the presence of all peoples." | And Simeon blessed them and said to Mary His mother, "Behold, this Child is set for the fall and rising of many in Israel. | And a sword will pierce through your own soul also, that thoughts out of many hearts may be revealed." | They returned into Galilee, to their own city, Nazareth. And the Child grew and became strong, filled with wisdom; and the favor of God was upon Him.

The Presentation

Ten simple reflections

The Holy Family

- The Holy Family's religious life was that of a Jewish family obedient to the law (*CCC*, 31).
- Joseph's offering was a poor man's alternative to a lamb. God wants me to sacrifice even in small things, too.

Simeon

- Some Eastern Churches call this mystery The Encounter in the Temple. Simeon and Anna come face-to-face with the Lord they have awaited (*CCC*, 529).
- Simeon's faith allowed him to recognize Christ.
- Simeon was content after one glimpse of Christ. The Eucharist gives me many glimpses.
- Trust in God's promises sustained Simeon.
- "The sword of sorrow predicted for Mary announces Christ's cross" (*CCC*, 529). Simeon foretells the Cross of Jesus—and suffering for His followers.

...and blessed is the fruit of thy womb, Jesus,
whom you presented in the Temple.

Mary, Our Model

- I should present Christ in the "temple of the Holy Spirit," my body.
- This encounter with Christ takes place in the Temple. For us, it happens in the Church.
- Anna, in the scene that follows this passage, "talked about the Child to all." My encounters with Christ should lead to evangelization.

Pray for me, Mary, cause of our joy,
that I will always be ready to encounter Christ.

THE FIFTH JOYFUL MYSTERY
The Finding in the Temple

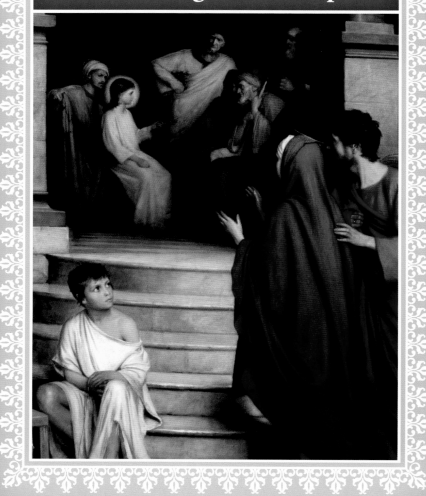

Mary and Joseph find
Jesus in the Temple.

FRUIT OF THE MYSTERY

That I will always look for Jesus in the Church
when I have lost Him in my life.

Ten verses from Luke 2:41-51. Now His parents went to Jerusalem every year at the Feast of the Passover. | And when He was twelve years old, they went up according to custom. | As they were returning, the Boy Jesus stayed behind in Jerusalem. His parents did not know it, | but supposing Him to be in the company they went a day's journey, and they sought Him among their kinsfolk and acquaintances. | And when they did not find Him, they returned to Jerusalem, seeking Him. |After three days they found Him in the Temple, sitting among the teachers, listening to them and asking questions; | and all who heard Him were amazed at His understanding and His answers. | And when they saw Him they were astonished; and His mother said to Him, "Son, why have you treated us so? Behold, Your father and I have been looking for You anxiously." | And He said to them, "How is it that you sought Me? Did you not know that I must be in My Father's house?" | And He went down with them and came to Nazareth, and was obedient to them; and His mother kept all these things in her heart.

The Finding in the Temple

Ten simple reflections

The Father

- Here Jesus lets us catch a glimpse of the mystery of His total consecration to His mission: "I must be about My Father's work" (*CCC*, 534).

- "Even the closest of human relationships are challenged by the absolute demands of the Kingdom" (Saint John Paul II, *Rosarium Virginis Mariae*, 20).

The Holy Family

- Joseph and Mary assumed Jesus was with members of their close-knit extended family in which cousins were "brothers."

- The Holy Family made a pilgrimage to Jerusalem every year. Do I take my family on special trips to holy places?

- "Jesus's obedience to His mother and legal father fulfills the Fourth Commandment perfectly and mirrors His obedience to His Father in Heaven" (*CCC*, 532).

- In the hidden years of Jesus we learn the importance of silence, family life, work, and the ordinary events of daily life (*CCC*, 533).

...and blessed is the fruit of thy womb, Jesus,
whom you found in the Temple.

Jesus in the Eucharist

- Sometimes I feel like I have "lost" Christ. When that happens, I can always find Him in the tabernacle (and in Confession).
- Jesus imparts wisdom to the rabbis who listen in the Temple. He will give me wisdom if I spend time with Him in the tabernacle.

Mary, Our Model

- Mary's question is direct, simple, and honest: "Why have You done this to us?" Our prayers should be direct, simple, and honest.
- Joseph and Mary "do not understand" Jesus's answer, and yet they accept it (*CCC*, 534). Do I accept or demand to know it all up front?

Pray for me, Mary, cause of our joy,
that I will always look for Jesus in the Church
when I have lost Him in my life.

APOSTOLIC LETTER
Rosarium Virginis Mariae

AN EXCERPT ON
THE MYSTERIES OF LIGHT

Mysteries to be prayed on Thursday

(21.) Moving on from the infancy and the hidden life in Nazareth to the public life of Jesus, our contemplation brings us to those mysteries which may be called in a special way "Mysteries of Light." Certainly the whole mystery of Christ is a mystery of light. He is the "light of the world" (Jn 8:12). Yet this truth emerges in a special way during the years of His public life, when He proclaims the Gospel of the Kingdom.

Each of these mysteries is *a revelation of the Kingdom now present in the very person of Jesus.* The Baptism in the Jordan is first of all a Mystery of Light. Here, as Christ descends into the waters, the innocent One who became "sin" for our sake (cf. 2Corinthians 5:21), the heavens open wide and the voice of the Father declares Him the beloved Son (cf. Matthew 3:17 and parallels), while the Spirit descends on Him to invest Him with the mission that He is to carry out. Another Mystery of Light is the first of the signs, given at Cana (cf. John 2:1- 12), when Christ changes water into wine and opens the hearts of the disciples to faith, thanks to the intervention of Mary, the first among believers. Another Mystery of Light is the preaching by which Jesus proclaims the coming of the Kingdom of God, calls to conversion (cf. Mark 1:15) and forgives the sins of all who draw near to Him in humble trust (cf. Mark 2:3-13; Luke 7:47- 48): the inauguration of that ministry of mercy that He continues to exercise until the end of the world, particularly through the Sacrament of Reconciliation which He has entrusted to his Church (cf. John 20:22-23). The Mystery of Light *par excellence* is the Transfiguration, traditionally believed to have taken place on Mount Tabor. The glory of the Godhead shines forth from the face of Christ as the Father commands the astonished Apostles to "listen to Him" (cf. Luke 9:35 and parallels) and to prepare to experience with Him the agony of the Passion, so as to come with Him to the joy of the Resurrection and a life transfigured by the Holy Spirit. A final Mystery of Light is the Institution of the Eucharist, in which Christ offers His body and blood as food under the signs of bread and wine, and testifies "to the end" His love for humanity (Jn 13:1), for whose salvation He will offer Himself in sacrifice.

In these mysteries, apart from the Miracle at Cana, *the presence of Mary remains in the background*. The Gospels make only the briefest reference to her occasional presence at one moment or other during the preaching of Jesus (cf. Mak 3:31-5; John 2:12), and they give no indication that she was present at the Last Supper and the Institution of the Eucharist. Yet the role she assumed at Cana in some way accompanies Christ throughout His ministry. The revelation made directly by the Father at the Baptism in the Jordan and echoed by John the Baptist is placed upon Mary's lips at Cana, and it becomes the great maternal counsel which Mary addresses to the Church of every age: "Do whatever He tells you" (John 2:5). This counsel is a fitting introduction to the words and signs of Christ's public ministry and it forms the Marian foundation of all the "Mysteries of Light."

THE FIRST LUMINOUS MYSTERY
The Baptism of the Lord

Jesus is baptized by John in the Jordan River.

That I will be faithful to my baptismal vows.

Ten verses from Matthew 3:1-17, 4:1. In those days came John the Baptist, preaching, "Repent, for the Kingdom of Heaven is at hand." │ John wore a garment of camel's hair, and a leather girdle around his waist; and his food was locusts and wild honey. │ He said: "I baptize you with water for repentance, but He who is coming after me is mightier than I, whose sandals I am not worthy to carry; │ He will baptize you with the Holy Spirit and with fire." │ Then Jesus came from Galilee to the Jordan to John, to be baptized by him. │ John would have prevented Him, saying, "I need to be baptized by You, and do You come to me?" │ But Jesus answered him, "Let it be so now; for thus it is fitting for us to fulfill all righteousness." │ And when Jesus was baptized, He went up immediately from the water, and behold, the heavens were opened and He saw the Spirit of God descending like a dove, and alighting on Him; │ and lo, a voice from Heaven, saying, "This is My beloved Son, with Whom I am well pleased." │ Then Jesus was led up by the Spirit into the wilderness to be tempted by the devil.

The Baptism of the Lord

Ten simple reflections

John the Baptist

- John did not point to anything but Christ: he was created for that. That is what I was created for, too.
- For John, only Christ's standards mattered, not the world's. What are my priorities?
- People were attracted to John, despite his appearance, because of his fidelity to God and His principles.
- John is not afraid to challenge people to change, and so he betters their lives and is remembered by history.

Jesus Christ

- "The Baptism of Jesus is on His part the acceptance and inauguration of His mission as God's Suffering Servant" (*CCC*, 536).
- "Already He is coming to 'fulfill all righteousness,' that is, He is submitting Himself entirely to His Father's will" (*CCC*, 536).
- At the beginning, the Father consoles His Son with His voice. Later, He will face the Cross and hear no consolation.

...and blessed is the fruit of thy womb, Jesus,
baptized by John.

Each Christian

- "The Christian must . . . go down into the water with Jesus in order to rise with Him, be reborn of water and the Spirit so as to become the Father's beloved son in the Son and walk in newness of life" (*CCC*, 537).

- In Baptism, Christ "procured for us a 'shortcut' to salvation" (*CCC*, 518).

- Water is necessary for life; similarly, Baptism is necessary for eternal life. I should be anxious to give that life to others.

Pray for me, Mary, star of the New Evangelization,
that I will be faithful to my baptismal vows.

The Wedding Feast at Cana

Jesus performs His first public miracle at His mother's request.

FRUIT OF THE MYSTERY

That I will do whatever He tells me.

Ten verses from John 2:1-11. On the third day there was a marriage at Cana in Galilee, and the mother of Jesus was there. | Jesus also was invited to the marriage, with His disciples. |When the wine gave out, the mother of Jesus said to Him, "They have no wine." | And Jesus said to her, "O woman, what have you to do with Me? My hour has not yet come." |His mother said to the servants, "Do whatever He tells you." | Now six stone jars were standing there, for the Jewish rites of purification, each holding twenty or thirty gallons. | Jesus said to them, "Fill the jars with water." And they filled them up to the brim. | He said to them, "Now draw some out, and take it to the steward of the feast." So they took it. | When the steward tasted the water now become wine, [he said,] "Every man serves the good wine first; and when men have drunk freely, then the poor wine; but you have kept the good wine until now." | This, the first of His signs, Jesus did at Cana in Galilee, and manifested His glory; and His disciples believed in Him.

The Wedding Feast at Cana

Ten simple reflections

Mary

- Here we find "the great maternal counsel, which Mary addresses to the Church of every age: 'Do whatever He tells you'" (*Rosarium*, 21).

- From the beginning, Christ imparts the faith to His disciples through Mary, "the first among believers" (*Rosarium*, 21).

- If we bring our needs to Mary, she will take care of them with her Son.

Jesus

- "What is this to Me?" is not a rebuke. Jesus recognizes that public miracle will lead to His death.

- Jesus at Cana "gives a sign, in which He proclaims His hour, the hour of the wedding feast, the hour of union between God and man" (Pope Benedict XVI, *Homily*, September 11, 2006).

- Jesus "transforms the human wedding feast into an image of the divine wedding feast . . . in which He gives us every good thing, represented by the abundance of wine" (Pope Benedict XVI, *Homily*, September 11, 2006).

Add after "Jesus," in each Hail Mary

...and blessed is the fruit of thy womb, Jesus,
who revealed His glory at your request.

Us

- Jesus chose this for His first public miracle in part to show how much He loves marriage and family.
- Christ "revealed His glory" by making wine. He also reveals His glory to us by making what is ordinary in our life extraordinary.
- "His disciples began to believe in Him" based on this miracle. We see a greater miracle at each Mass.
- Christ announced His ministry in the Temple, then began it in Cana. My Christian mission is launched in the Church, but it takes place in the world.

Pray for me, Mary, star of the New Evangelization,
that I will do whatever He tells me.

The Proclamation of the Kingdom

Jesus announces the coming of the Kingdom and forgives sins.

FRUIT OF THE MYSTERY
That I will repent and enter the Kingdom.

Ten verses from the Book of Matthew. From that time Jesus began to preach, saying, "Repent, for the Kingdom of Heaven is at hand." │ And He went about all Galilee, teaching in their synagogues and preaching the Gospel of the Kingdom and healing every disease ... │ Seeing the crowds, He went up on the mountain, and when He sat down His disciples came to Him. │ And He opened His mouth and taught them, saying: "Blessed are the poor in spirit, for theirs is the Kingdom of Heaven." │ "Blessed are those who are persecuted for righteousness' sake, for theirs is the Kingdom of Heaven." │ "Not everyone who says to Me, 'Lord, Lord,' shall enter the Kingdom of Heaven, but he who does the will of My Father who is in Heaven." │ To Peter: "I will give you the keys of the Kingdom of Heaven, and whatever you bind on earth shall be bound in Heaven, and whatever you loose on earth shall be loosed in Heaven." │ "Truly, I say to you, unless you turn and become like children, you will never enter the Kingdom of Heaven." │ "Again I tell you, it is easier for a camel to go through the eye of a needle than for a rich man to enter the Kingdom of God." │ "And this Gospel of the Kingdom will be preached throughout the whole world, as a testimony to all nations."

The Proclamation of the Kingdom

Ten simple reflections

The King

● "The Kingdom of Heaven was inaugurated on earth by Jesus. . . . The Church is the seed and beginning of this Kingdom. Its keys are entrusted to Peter" (*CCC*, 567).

● Christ's whole early life—His words and deeds, His silences and sufferings; indeed, His manner of being and speaking—tell us who God is and what He is like (*CCC*, 561).

The Invitation

● Jesus invites sinners to the table of the Kingdom" (*CCC*, 545) and "forgives the sins of all who draw near Him in humble trust" (*Rosarium*, 21).

● "Everyone is called to enter the Kingdom" (*CCC*, 543).

● "One must enter the Kingdom, that is, become a disciple of Christ, in order to 'know its secrets.'" It is hard to understand for those outside it (*CCC*, 546).

● Praying "Thy Kingdom come" "means working to enrich American society and culture with the beauty and truth of the Gospel" (Pope Benedict XVI, *Mass at Yankee Stadium*, April 20, 2008).

...and blessed is the fruit of thy womb, Jesus,
proclaiming the Kingdom and forgiving sins.

The Response

- "To become a child in relation to God is the condition for entering the Kingdom. For this, we must humble ourselves and become little" (*CCC*, 561).
- I pray "Thy Kingdom come," but the next part of the Our Father demands something of me: "Thy will be done."
- "There is no human activity—even in secular affairs—which can be withdrawn from God's dominion" (*Lumen Gentium*, 36).
- Jesus is King of everything: truth, my leisure time, the business world, my family. Do I let Him reign?

Pray for me, Mary, star of the New Evangelization,
that I will repent and enter the Kingdom.

THE FOURTH LUMINOUS MYSTERY
The Transfiguration

Jesus is transfigured,
dazzling white, on Mount Tabor.

FRUIT OF THE MYSTERY
That I will always listen to Jesus.

Ten verses from Matthew 17:1-8. And after six days Jesus took with Him Peter and James and John his brother, and led them up a high mountain apart. | And He was transfigured before them, and His face shone like the sun, and His garments became white as light. | And behold, there appeared to them Moses and Elijah, talking with Him. | And Peter said to Jesus, "Lord, it is well that we are here; if You wish, I will make three booths here, one for You and one for Moses and one for Elijah." | He was still speaking, when lo, a bright cloud overshadowed them, and a voice from the cloud said, "This is My beloved Son, with Whom I am well pleased; listen to Him." | When the disciples heard this, they fell on their faces, and were filled with awe. | But Jesus came and touched them, saying, "Rise, and have no fear." And when they lifted up their eyes, they saw no one but Jesus only. | **From 2 Peter 1:16-18:** We did not follow cleverly devised myths when we made known to you the power and coming of Our Lord Jesus Christ, but we were eyewitnesses of His majesty. | When He received honor and glory from God the Father and the voice was borne to Him by the Majestic Glory, "This is My beloved Son, with whom I am well pleased …" | We heard this voice borne from Heaven, for we were with Him on the holy mountain.

The Transfiguration

Ten simple reflections

Jesus

- "For a moment Jesus discloses His divine glory, confirming Peter's confession" (*CCC*, 555).

- The light of the sun is the most intense ever known in nature. But the disciples saw a brightness more intense: the divine glory of Jesus (cf. Pope Benedict XVI, *Angelus*, March 20, 2011).

- "Christ's Transfiguration aims at strengthening the Apostles' faith in anticipation of His passion: The ascent on the high mountain prepares for the ascent to Calvary" (*CCC*, 568).

The Cross

- "Moses and Elijah had seen God's glory on the mountain; the law and the prophets had announced the Messiah's sufferings" (*CCC*, 555).

- "The whole Trinity appeared: the Father in the voice, the Son in the man, the Spirit in the shining cloud" (*CCC*, 555).

- "The Transfiguration gives us a foretaste of Christ's glorious coming . . . But it also recalls that 'it is through many persecutions that we must enter the Kingdom of God'" (*CCC*, 556).

...and blessed is the fruit of thy womb, Jesus,
transfigured on Mount Tabor.

The Apostles

- The three Apostles were rewarded for saying yes to Christ's invitation, praying, and staying close to Him.
- They saw who Christ really was and so will we if we follow Him closely and pray.
- Think of the Transfiguration when praying the Glory Be prayer.
- If your love for God is cold, remember when it was fresh and exciting so your passion will return.

Pray for me, Mary, star of the New Evangelization,
that I will always listen to Jesus.

At the Last Supper, Christ changes bread and wine into His Body and Blood.

FRUIT OF THE MYSTERY
That my desire for holiness will grow.

Ten verses from First Corinthians 11:23-29.   For I received from the Lord what I also delivered to you, that the Lord Jesus on the night when He was betrayed took bread | and when He had given thanks, He broke it, and said, "This is My Body, which is for you. Do this in remembrance of Me." | In the same way also the cup, after supper, saying, "This cup is the new covenant in My Blood. Do this, as often as you drink it, in remembrance of Me." | For as often as you eat this bread and drink the cup, you proclaim the Lord's death until He comes. | Whoever, therefore, eats the bread or drinks the cup of the Lord in an unworthy manner will be guilty of profaning the Body and Blood of the Lord. | Let a man examine himself, and so eat of the bread and drink of the cup. | For anyone who eats and drinks without discerning the Body eats and drinks judgment upon himself. | **From John 6:** Jesus said to them: "I am the living Bread, which came down from Heaven; if any one eats of this Bread, he will live forever; and the Bread which I shall give for the life of the world is My Flesh." | "He who eats My Flesh and drinks My Blood abides in Me, and I in him." | After this many of His disciples drew back and no longer went about with Him.

The Institution of the Eucharist

Ten simple reflections

The Lord

- God said, "Let there be light." And there was. Here He says, "This is My Body." And it is.

- "Jesus freely offered Himself for our salvation. During the Last Supper, He both symbolized this offering and made it really present" (*CCC*, 621).

- "Jesus includes the Apostles in His own offering and bids them perpetuate it. By doing so, the Lord institutes His Apostles as priests" (*CCC*, 611).

The Church

- Eleven of Christ's first twelve priests betrayed or abandoned Him.

- Pope Benedict XVI called the Eucharist "a gift of love that is truly worth more than all the rest of life" (*Catechesis for Children Who Received First Communion*, October 15, 2005).

- Through real communion with His Body and Blood, "Christ enables us to live in Him all that He Himself lived, and He lives it in us" (*CCC*, 521).

Add after "Jesus," in each Hail Mary

...and blessed is the fruit of thy womb, Jesus,
who offers Himself to me in the Eucharist.

The Mass

- Heaven is like a big, joyous wedding feast. And it starts at Mass.
- If I were given a hammer and nails, or a sword, at Mass, the message would be obvious: build something, or fight. I'm given Christ. I am to bring Him to the world.
- Christ is present in the Eucharist whether I feel His presence or not—but if I forgive more, pray more, and serve more, I will "feel" His presence more, too.
- The Eucharist is the encounter with Christ par excellence. Who was the last person I invited back to Mass?

Pray for me, Mary, star of the New Evangelization,
that my desire for holiness will grow.

APOSTOLIC LETTER
Rosarium Virginis Mariae

AN EXCERPT ON
THE SORROWFUL MYSTERIES

Mysteries to be prayed on Tuesday and Friday

(22.) The Gospels give great prominence to the Sorrowful Mysteries of Christ. From the beginning, Christian piety, especially during the Lenten devotion of the *Way of the Cross*, has focused on the individual moments of the Passion, realizing that here is found *the culmination of the revelation of God's love* and the source of our salvation. The Rosary selects certain moments from the Passion, inviting the faithful to contemplate them in their hearts and to relive them. The sequence of meditations begins with Gethsemane, where Christ experiences a moment of great anguish before the will of the Father, against which the weakness of the flesh would be tempted to rebel. There Jesus encounters all the temptations and confronts all the sins of humanity, in order to say to the Father: "Not My will but Yours be done" (Luke 22:42 and parallels). This "yes" of Christ reverses the "no" of our first parents in the Garden of Eden. And the cost of this faithfulness to the Father's will is made clear in the following mysteries: by His scourging, His crowning with thorns, His carrying the Cross, and His death on the Cross, the Lord is cast into the most abject suffering: *Ecce homo!*

This abject suffering reveals not only the love of God but also the meaning of man himself.

Ecce homo: the meaning, origin, and fulfillment of man is to be found in Christ, the God who humbles Himself out of love "even unto death, death on a cross" (Phil 2:8). The Sorrowful Mysteries help the believer to relive the death of Jesus, to stand at the foot of the Cross beside Mary, to enter with her into the depths of God's love for man and to experience all its life-giving power.

The Agony in the Garden

Jesus prays in Gethsemane
on the night before His death.

FRUIT OF THE MYSTERY
That I will have a faith that is humble and obedient.

Ten verses from Luke 22:39-48. And He came out, and went, as was His custom, to the Mount of Olives; and the disciples followed Him. | And when He came to the place He said to them, "Pray that you may not enter into temptation." | And He withdrew from them about a stone's throw, and knelt down and prayed, | "Father, if Thou art willing, remove this cup from Me; nevertheless not My will, but Thine, be done." | And there appeared to Him an angel from Heaven, strengthening Him. | And being in an agony He prayed more earnestly; and His sweat became like great drops of blood falling down upon the ground. | And when He rose from prayer, He came to the disciples and found them sleeping for sorrow, | and He said to them, "Why do you sleep? Rise and pray that you may not enter into temptation." | While He was still speaking, there came a crowd, and the man called Judas, one of the twelve, was leading them. He drew near to Jesus to kiss Him; | but Jesus said to him, "Judas, would you betray the Son of Man with a kiss?"

The Agony in the Garden

Ten simple reflections

Jesus

- Jesus "expresses the horror that death represented for His human nature" (*CCC*, 612).
- "By accepting in His human will that the Father's will be done, He accepts His death as redemptive" (*CCC*, 612).
- This yes of Christ reverses the no of our first parents in the Garden of Eden (*Rosarium*, 22).
- In Gethsemane, "Jesus encounters all the temptations and confronts all the sins of humanity" (*Rosarium*, 22).

The Eucharist

- "Could you not stay one hour with Me?" Christ would like us to make a Holy Hour in the presence of the Eucharist (weekly, if possible).
- "The cup of the New Covenant, which Jesus offered at the Last Supper, is afterward accepted by Him from His Father's hands in His agony of the garden" (*CCC*, 612).

...and blessed is the fruit of thy womb, Jesus,
in agony for me.

- The disciples disobey Christ's command not because they are "wicked" but because they give in to their desire for easy comfort. That is often the reason I sin.

Obedience

- The everyday obedience of Jesus to Joseph and Mary both announced and anticipated the obedience of Holy Thursday (*CCC*, 532).
- "Father, if you are willing . . ." It is no shame to pray, and hope for, pain to pass me by . . .
- "Still, not My will but Yours"—I should remember that sometimes God wants me to accept suffering for a greater purpose.

Pray for me, Mary, Mother of Sorrows,
that I will have a faith that is humble and obedient.

The Scourging at the Pillar

Christ is scourged by the soldiers at Pilate's command.

FRUIT OF THE MYSTERY

That I will have a love that accepts suffering and setback.

Ten Verses; From Mark 15:6-15: Now at the feast he used to release for them one prisoner for whom they asked. | And he answered them, "Do you want me to release for you the King of the Jews?" | For he perceived that it was out of envy that the chief priests had delivered Him up. | But the chief priests stirred up the crowd to have him release for them Barabbas [a murderer] instead. | And Pilate again said to them, "Then what shall I do with the Man whom you call the King of the Jews?" And they cried out again, "Crucify Him." | And Pilate said to them, "Why, what evil has He done?" But they shouted all the more, "Crucify Him." | So Pilate, wishing to satisfy the crowd, released for them Barabbas; and having scourged Jesus, he delivered Him to be crucified. | **From 1 Peter 2:21-25:** Christ also suffered for you, leaving you an example, that you should follow in His steps. | He committed no sin; no guile was found on His lips. | When He was reviled, He did not revile in return; when He suffered, He did not threaten; but He trusted to Him who judges justly. | By His wounds you have been healed.

The Scourging at the Pillar

Ten simple reflections

The Passion

- The kind of scourges used on Christ included three leather whips held together by a handle. At the ends were spiky pieces of bone or lead.
- Roman scourges would tear away flesh and the victim would lose blood, weakening him for crucifixion. The soldiers avoided striking over the heart, to keep the condemned man alive.
- In the garden, Heaven's help was obvious—an angel. In the scourging, the interior grace of hope is Jesus's only help. I can expect the same sometimes.

Our Sins

- "[T]he Church does not hesitate to impute to Christians the gravest responsibility for the torments inflicted upon Jesus" (*CCC*, 598).
- "Christ's whole life was lived under the sign of persecution. His own share it with Him" (*CCC*, 530).
- That the manner of His death was foreseen "does not mean that those who handed Him over were merely passive players in a scenario written in advance by God" (*CCC*, 599).

...and blessed is the fruit of thy womb, Jesus,
scourged for me.

Our Response

- If He suffered this for me, there is nothing I should refuse to do for Him.
- Consider small "scourges" to suffer for love of Christ. Eating and not getting quite full? Sacrificing dessert or screen time?
- When I give in to angry or vengeful thoughts and make cutting remarks or judgmental gossip, I behave like the soldiers.
- When I leave cutting remarks unanswered or let judgmental thoughts die in my mind, I behave like Christ.

Pray for me, Mary, Mother of Sorrows,
that I will have a love that accepts suffering and setback.

The Crowning with Thorns

Soldiers weave a crown of thorns and place it on Christ's head.

FRUIT OF THE MYSTERY
That I will seek fidelity above honor.

Ten verses from John 18:36-19:14. Jesus answered, "My Kingship is not of this world; if My Kingship were of this world, My servants would fight, that I might not be handed over to the Jews; but My Kingship is not from the world. | For this I was born, and for this I have come into the world, to bear witness to the truth. Everyone who is of the truth hears My voice." | Pilate said to Him, "What is truth?" | And the soldiers plaited a crown of thorns, and put it on His head, and arrayed Him in a purple robe; | they came up to Him, saying, "Hail, King of the Jews!" and struck Him with their hands. | So Jesus came out, wearing the crown of thorns and the purple robe. Pilate said to them, "Behold the Man!" | He entered the praetorium again and said to Jesus, . . . "Do You not know that I have power to release You, and power to crucify You?" | Jesus answered him, "You would have no power over Me unless it had been given you from above." | Upon this Pilate sought to release Him, but the Jews cried out, "If you release this Man, you are not Caesar's friend; everyone who makes himself a king sets himself against Caesar." | When Pilate heard these words, he brought Jesus out and sat down on the judgment seat. | He said to the Jews, "Behold your King!"

The Crowning with Thorns

Ten simple reflections

Jesus

- "Jesus atoned for our faults and made satisfaction for our sins to the Father (*CCC*, 615).
- "There is not, never has been, and never will be a single human being for whom Christ did not suffer" (*CCC*, 605).
- The blood vessels in the face bleed profusely. The crown of thorns made it difficult for Christ to see.

The Crowd

- That there was something special about Christ was obvious to many at a glance. This is what gave the soldiers their delight when they mocked Him.
- When He fed the multitudes, they wanted to make Him King. But thorns were the only crown He accepted.
- We might avoid talking about Jesus because we are afraid of ridicule. But without risking ridicule, we will never fully imitate Christ.

Add after "Jesus," in each Hail Mary

...and blessed is the fruit of thy womb, Jesus,
crowned with thorns.

Our Response

- The crown of thorns is an antidote to self-pity, to prevent me crowning myself for my own slight sufferings.
- Empty religious practice is like crowning Christ with thorns.
- Giving a deep, honest, thorough Confession is one way to imitate Christ, who exposed Himself to contempt.
- Even the Rosary can be an empty crown if I "say" it without trying to "pray" it.

Pray for me, Mary, Mother of Sorrows,
that I will seek fidelity above honor.

The Carrying of the Cross

Jesus struggles up Calvary with His own Cross on His shoulders.

FRUIT OF THE MYSTERY

That I will have perseverance as I take up my cross each day.

Ten Verses; From John 19:17: And carrying the Cross Himself, He went out to what is called the Place of the Skull, in Hebrew, Golgotha. | **From Luke 23:26-31:** And as they led Him away, they seized one Simon of Cyrene, who was coming in from the country, and laid on him the Cross, to carry it behind Jesus. | And there followed Him a great multitude of the people, and of women who bewailed and lamented Him. | But Jesus turning to them said, "Daughters of Jerusalem, do not weep for Me, but weep for yourselves and for your children. | For behold, the days are coming when they will say, 'Blessed are the barren, and the wombs that never bore, and the breasts that never gave suck!' | Then they will begin to say to the mountains, 'Fall on us'; and to the hills, 'Cover us.' | For if they do this when the wood is green, what will happen when it is dry?" | **From Matthew 16:24-26:** Then Jesus told His disciples, "If any man would come after Me, let him deny himself and take up his Cross and follow Me. | For whoever would save his life will lose it, and whoever loses his life for My sake will find it. | For what will it profit a man, if he gains the whole world and forfeits his life? Or what shall a man give in return for his life?"

The Carrying of the Cross

Ten simple reflections

Jesus

- Jesus accepted His heavy Cross without professing His innocence —because He was carrying it for the guilty. For me.
- It is easy to imagine Jesus struggling in front of our admiring eyes. But, abandoned by His friends and rejected by the crowd, it's truer to think of Him being alone.
- Jesus was a strong man. He fell three times, tradition tells us. Sleepless, scourged, crowned with thorns, and carrying a heavy cross, He kept getting back up.

The Faithful Ones

- It was horrible for Mary to have to watch this; she would rather she were allowed to suffer it herself.
- In the stories of Simon and Veronica, we see that Christ accepted the assistance of others as He redeemed the world.
- The Blessed Mother of Jesus was close when her Son was suffering. She is close when we, her other sons and daughters, suffer.

Add after "Jesus," in each Hail Mary

...and blessed is the fruit of thy womb, Jesus,
carrying His Cross.

- Remember "the martyrs of our own time," Pope Francis suggests. "They refuse to deny Jesus, and they endure insult and injury with dignity. They follow Him on His way" (*Palm Sunday Homily*, March 29, 2015).

My Cross
- The cross I have been given has been hand-tested by Christ so that it will be neither too heavy—nor too light.
- Christ carries His Cross—and helps carry mine as well.
- Am I sick of trying to be holy and always failing? My struggle for holiness, with all of its falls, is my lifelong Way of the Cross.

Pray for me, Mary, Mother of Sorrows,
that I will have perseverance as I take up my cross each day.

The Crucifixion

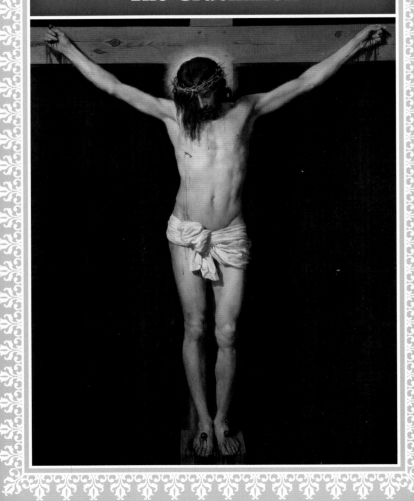

Jesus is nailed to the Cross and dies.

FRUIT OF THE MYSTERY

That I will crucify my pride with Christ on the Cross.

Ten verses from Mark 15:24-39. And they crucified Him, and divided His garments among them, casting lots for them, to decide what each should take. And it was the third hour, when they crucified Him. | And the inscription of the charge against Him read, "The King of the Jews." | And with Him they crucified two robbers, one on His right and one on His left. | So also the chief priests mocked Him to one another with the scribes, saying . . . | "Let the Christ, the King of Israel, come down now from the Cross, that we may see and believe." | And when the sixth hour had come, there was darkness over the whole land until the ninth hour. | And at the ninth hour Jesus cried with a loud voice, "E'lo-i, E'lo-i, la'ma sabach-tha'ni?" which means, "My God, My God, why hast Thou forsaken Me?" | And Jesus uttered a loud cry, and breathed His last. | And the curtain of the Temple was torn in two, from top to bottom. | And when the centurion, who stood facing Him, saw that He thus breathed His last, he said, "Truly this Man was the Son of God!"

The Crucifixion

Ten simple reflections

Christ's Sacrifice

- It took a great effort for Jesus to speak from the Cross; He had to raise Himself up on His wounded hands. Yet He did—to forgive.
- "It is love 'to the end' that confers on Christ's sacrifice its value as redemption and reparation, as atonement and satisfaction" (*CCC*, 616).
- "He knew and loved us all when He offered His life" (*CCC*, 616).
- Jesus died for the very people who were mocking Him, blaspheming Him—and killing Him.

Our Sin

- "Since our sins made the Lord Jesus Christ suffer the torment of the Cross, those who plunge themselves into disorders and crimes crucify the Son of God anew" (*CCC*, 598).
- "Apart from the Cross there is no other ladder by which we may get to Heaven" (*CCC*, 618).
- The Crucifix teaches us about God's mercy—but also about His anger at sin. We must remember both.

...and blessed is the fruit of thy womb, Jesus,
crucified for me.

Our Response

- To crucify my pride is necessary for me, because I am by nature egotistical and prone to hurt others selfishly.
- To imitate Christ's forgiveness is necessary for me, because those I am close with are by nature egotistical and prone to hurt me selfishly.
- The Church, following the Apostles, teaches that Christ died for all men without exception (*CCC*, 605).

Pray for me, Mary, Mother of Sorrows,
that I will crucify my pride with Christ on the Cross.

APOSTOLIC LETTER
Rosarium Virginis Mariae

AN EXCERPT ON
THE GLORIOUS MYSTERIES

Mysteries to be prayed on Wednesday and Sunday

(23.) "The contemplation of Christ's face cannot stop at the image of the Crucified One. He is the Risen One!" The Rosary has always expressed this knowledge born of faith and invited the believer to pass beyond the darkness of the Passion in order to gaze upon Christ's glory in the Resurrection and Ascension. Contemplating the Risen One, Christians *rediscover the reasons for their own faith* (cf. 1 Corinthians 15:14) and relive the joy not only of those to whom Christ appeared—the Apostles, Mary Magdalene, and the disciples on the road to Emmaus—but also *the joy of Mary*, who must have had an equally intense experience of the new life of her glorified Son. In the Ascension, Christ was raised in glory to the right hand of the Father, while Mary herself would be raised to that same glory in the Assumption, enjoying beforehand, by a unique privilege, the destiny reserved for all the just at the resurrection of the dead. Crowned in glory—as she appears in the last Glorious Mystery—Mary shines forth as Queen of the Angels and Saints, the anticipation and the supreme realization of the eschatological state of the Church.

At the center of this unfolding sequence of the glory of the Son and the Mother, the Rosary sets before us the third Glorious Mystery, Pentecost, which reveals the face of the Church as a family gathered together with Mary, enlivened by the powerful outpouring of the Spirit and ready for the mission of evangelization. The contemplation of this scene, like that of the other Glorious Mysteries, ought to lead the faithful to an ever-greater appreciation of their new life in Christ, lived in the heart of the Church, a life of which the scene of Pentecost itself is the great "icon." The Glorious Mysteries thus lead the faithful to *greater hope for the eschatological goal* toward which they journey as members of the pilgrim People of God in history. This can only impel them to bear courageous witness to that "good news" that gives meaning to their entire existence.

The Resurrection

Jesus rises from the dead
three days after His crucifixion.

FRUIT OF THE MYSTERY

That hope in the risen Christ will drive out my cowardice.

Ten verses from Matthew 28:1-10. Now after the Sabbath, toward the dawn of the first day of the week, Mary Magdalene and the other Mary went to see the sepulchre. | And behold, there was a great earthquake; for an angel of the Lord descended from Heaven and came and rolled back the stone, and sat upon it. | His appearance was like lightning, and his raiment white as snow. | And for fear of him the guards trembled and became like dead men. | But the angel said to the women, "Do not be afraid; for I know that you seek Jesus who was crucified. | He is not here; for He has risen, as He said. Come, see the place where He lay. | Then go quickly and tell His disciples that He has risen from the dead, and behold, He is going before you to Galilee; there you will see Him. Lo, I have told you." | So they departed quickly from the tomb with fear and great joy, and ran to tell His disciples. | And behold, Jesus met them and said, "Hail!" And they came up and took hold of His feet and worshipped Him. | Then Jesus said to them, "Do not be afraid; go and tell My brethren to go to Galilee, and there they will see Me."

The Resurrection

Ten simple reflections

A Real Event

- Christ's resurrection is a real event that was historically verified (*CCC*, 639).

- The faith of the first Christians in the Resurrection was based on the witness of concrete men living among them. Paul speaks clearly of more than five-hundred to whom Jesus appeared on a single occasion (*CCC*, 642).

- Even when faced with the reality of the risen Jesus the disciples are still doubtful, so impossible did the thing seem. It doesn't make sense to say the Apostles believed the Resurrection because they were gullible (*CCC*, 644).

The Resurrected Christ

- "Mary must have had an intense experience of the new life of her glorified Son" (*Rosarium*, 23).

- Risen, Jesus can be touched. He eats. Yet His risen Body is not limited by space and time—Christ's resurrection was not a return to earthly life (*CCC*, 646).

- Christ, risen, still bears His wounds. You can't have Christ without the Crucifix.

...and blessed is the fruit of thy womb, Jesus,
who conquered death.

My Faith

- Do I think of the Resurrection like a fairy tale? If it isn't literally true, Christianity is wicked—the Cross without redemption.
- The women who visited the tomb were so filled with joy, they ran to tell the others. My encounter with Christ should be that real.
- Christ's appearance on the road to Emmaus is like Mass. He tells the disciples about the Scriptures, breaks bread, then disappears. The message: we must now seek Him in the Eucharist.
- Sunday is the feast of the Resurrection, the Lord's Day. How do I make it holy?

Pray for me, Mary, gate of Heaven,
that hope in the risen Christ will drive out my cowardice.

THE SECOND GLORIOUS MYSTERY
The Ascension

Forty days after rising from the dead, Christ ascends into Heaven.

FRUIT OF THE MYSTERY

That I will fulfill Christ's command to evangelize.

Ten Verses; From Matthew 28:16-20: Now the eleven disciples went to Galilee, to the mountain to which Jesus had directed them. | And when they saw Him they worshipped Him; but some doubted. | And Jesus came and said to them, "All authority in Heaven and on earth has been given to Me. | Go therefore and make disciples of all nations, baptizing them in the name of the Father and of the Son and of the Holy Spirit | teaching them to observe all that I have commanded you; and lo, I am with you always, to the close of the age." | **From Acts 1:8-11:** Jesus said: "You shall receive power when the Holy Spirit has come upon you; | and you shall be My witnesses in Jerusalem and in all Judea and Samaria and to the end of the earth." | And when He had said this, as they were looking on, He was lifted up, and a cloud took Him out of their sight. | And while they were gazing into Heaven as He went, behold, two men stood by them in white robes | and said, "Men of Galilee, why do you stand looking into Heaven? This Jesus, who was taken up from you into Heaven, will come in the same way as you saw Him go into Heaven."

The Ascension

Ten simple reflections

The Ascension

- "Jesus's final apparition ends with the irreversible entry of His humanity into divine glory . . . where He is seated from that time forward at God's right hand" (*CCC*, 659).

- "Only the One who 'came from the Father' can return to the Father: Christ Jesus" (*CCC*, 661).

- We have faith, because Christ is seated at the right hand of the Father. We have hope, because we know all authority is His. We have love, because He has entrusted us with so much.

Christ's Authority

- Before the Ascension, Christ was to be found on earth, always in one place. Now we can find Him anywhere.

- "All authority in Heaven and on earth is given to Me." We can have great confidence that, with Christ, we are on the winning team.

- All authority has been given to Christ. That means over every aspect of my life.

...and blessed is the fruit of thy womb, Jesus,
who ascended into Heaven.

- We can imagine that Mary would have told the Apostles to "do whatever He tells you" after Jesus's ascension, when she joined them in awaiting the Holy Spirit (*Rosarium*, 14).

Our Mission

- By telling the Apostles to convert the nations and then departing, Christ's message was obvious: we are to do His work now.
- "Why are you standing there looking at the sky?" Christianity isn't stargazing—it's serving, praying, and acting in this world.
- Christ will return in the same way. Am I ready?

Pray for me, Mary, gate of Heaven,
that I will fulfill Christ's command to evangelize.

The Descent of the Holy Spirit

The Holy Spirit descends on Mary and the Apostles.

That I will allow the Holy Spirit to overcome me.

Ten verses from Acts 2:1-6, 14-18. When the day of Pentecost had come, they were all together in one place. | And suddenly a sound came from Heaven like the rush of a mighty wind, and it filled all the house where they were sitting. | And there appeared to them tongues as of fire, distributed and resting on each one of them. | And they were all filled with the Holy Spirit and began to speak in other tongues, as the Spirit gave them utterance. | Now there were dwelling in Jerusalem Jews, devout men from every nation under Heaven. | And at this sound the multitude came together, and they were bewildered, because each one heard them speaking in his own language. | But Peter, standing with the eleven, lifted up his voice and addressed them: | "Men of Judea and all who dwell in Jerusalem, let this be known to you, and give ear to my words. | This is what was spoken by the prophet Joel: | 'And in the last days it shall be, God declares, that I will pour out My Spirit upon all flesh, and your sons and your daughters shall prophesy.'"

The Descent of the Holy Spirit

Ten simple reflections

The Holy Spirit

- On that Pentecost, the Holy Trinity is fully revealed (*CCC*, 732).
- The Bible itself says that only a small portion of Christ's teaching is contained in it. The rest is given to the Church through the Holy Spirit (cf. John 21:25).
- "By His coming, which never ceases, the Holy Spirit causes the world to enter into the 'last days,' the time of the Church" (*CCC*, 732).
- We know the Holy Spirit: in the Scriptures He inspired, in the Tradition, in the Church's Magisterium, in the sacramental liturgy, in prayer, in the charisms and ministries by which the Church is built up, in apostolic and missionary life, in the witness of saints (*CCC*, 688).

The Mission

- "Through the Holy Spirit we are restored to paradise, led back to the Kingdom of Heaven and adopted as children, given confidence to call God 'Father' and to share in Christ's grace, called children of light and given a share in eternal glory" (*CCC*, 736).

Add after "Jesus," in each Hail Mary

...and blessed is the fruit of thy womb, Jesus,
who pours forth His Holy Spirit.

- Christ is a teacher, model, savior. The Holy Spirit is our animating principle, our partner.
- The seven gifts of the Holy Spirit are wisdom, understanding, counsel, fortitude, knowledge, piety, and fear of the Lord (*CCC*, 1831).

My Life

- The Holy Spirit turned the cowardly Apostles into fearless martyrs. He will transform me, too.
- All heard the Apostles in their own language. The Holy Spirit can help me overcome interpersonal difficulties I have.
- The Holy Spirit was poured out on me starting at Baptism. Have I squandered this great gift? Or learned to use it?

Pray for me, Mary, gate of Heaven,
that I will allow the Holy Spirit to overcome me.

At the end of her life, Mary is taken body and soul into Heaven.

That I will follow Mary to Heaven, bringing others with me.

Ten verses from Revelation 12:1-10. And a great portent appeared in Heaven, a woman clothed with the sun, with the moon under her feet, and on her head a crown of twelve stars; | she was with child and she cried out in her pangs of birth, in anguish for delivery. | And another portent appeared in Heaven; behold, a great red dragon, with seven heads and ten horns, and seven diadems upon his heads. | His tail swept down a third of the stars of Heaven, and cast them to the earth. | And the dragon stood before the woman who was about to bear a child, that he might devour her child when she brought it forth; | she brought forth a male Child, one who is to rule all the nations with a rod of iron, but her Child was caught up to God and to His throne, | and the woman fled into the wilderness, where she has a place prepared by God. | Now war arose in Heaven, Michael and his angels fighting against the dragon; and the dragon and his angels fought | but they were defeated and there was no longer any place for them in Heaven. | And I heard a loud voice in Heaven, saying, "Now the salvation and the power and the Kingdom of our God and the authority of His Christ have come."

The Assumption

Ten simple reflections

Mary

- "The Most Blessed Virgin Mary, when the course of her earthly life was completed, was taken up body and soul into the glory of Heaven" (*CCC*, 974).

- In Heaven, Mary "already shares in the glory of her Son's resurrection, anticipating the resurrection of all members of His body" (*CCC*, 974).

- Mary "shines forth on earth until the day of the Lord shall come, a sign of certain hope and comfort to the pilgrim people of God" (*CCC*, 972).

- "The Father blessed Mary more than any other created person 'in Christ with every spiritual blessing in the heavenly places'" (*CCC*, 492).

- The mother of Jesus, "in the glory which she possesses in body and soul in Heaven, is the image and beginning of the Church as it is to be perfected in the world to come" (*CCC*, 972).

Jesus

- "What the Catholic faith believes about Mary is based on what it believes about Christ" (*CCC*, 487).

...and blessed is the fruit of thy womb, Jesus,
who assumed you into Heaven.

- Mary was, "from the first moment of her conception, by a singular grace and privilege of Almighty God and by virtue of the merits of Jesus Christ, Savior of the human race, preserved immune from all stain of original sin" (Catechism, 487).
- "To become the mother of the Savior, Mary was enriched by God with gifts appropriate to such a role" (*CCC*, 490).

Our Response

- At the end of time, "the universe itself will be renewed." There in "a new heavens and a new earth" all the righteous will dwell "for ever with Christ, glorified in body and soul" (CCC, 1042).
- In Heaven the blessed live "in Christ," but "retain, or rather find, their true identity, their own name" given by God (CCC 1025, Revelation 2:17).

Pray for me, Mary, gate of Heaven,
that I will follow Mary to Heaven, bringing others with me.

The Coronation

Mary is crowned
Queen of Heaven and earth.

FRUIT OF THE MYSTERY

That I will trust in the intercession of Mary in my great need.

Ten verses from Luke 1:46-55. And Mary said, "My soul magnifies the Lord | and my spirit rejoices in God my Savior, | for He has regarded the low estate of His handmaiden. For behold, henceforth all generations will call me blessed; | for He who is mighty has done great things for me, and holy is His name. | And His mercy is on those who fear Him from generation to generation. | He has shown strength with His arm, He has scattered the proud in the imagination of their hearts, | He has put down the mighty from their thrones, and exalted those of low degree; | He has filled the hungry with good things, and the rich He has sent empty away. | He has helped his servant Israel, in remembrance of His mercy, | as He spoke to our fathers, to Abraham and to his posterity forever."

The Coronation

Ten simple reflections

The Queen

- "Since the fifth century, Christians have given Mary the title of queen in acknowledgment of her sublime dignity as the mother of God" (Saint John Paul II, *General Audience*, June 1997).

- Christians call Mary our queen also because of "her importance in the life of the Church and in the lives of individuals" (*General Audience*, 1997).

- The Second Vatican Council teaches that Mary "has been exalted by the Lord as queen of all, in order that she might be more fully conformed to her Son, the Lord of lords" (*Lumen Gentium*, 59).

- "Crowned in glory, Mary shines forth as queen of the angels and saints" (*Rosarium*, 23).

Her Subjects

- Mary is "the anticipation and the supreme realization of the heavenly state of the Church" (*Rosarium*, 23).

- "As the queen . . . Mary remains close to us at every step of our earthly pilgrimage, supporting us in our trials and sharing with us the life and love of Jesus her Son" (Saint John Paul II, June 1997).

Add after "Jesus," in each Hail Mary

...and blessed is the fruit of thy womb, Jesus,
who crowned you Queen of Heaven and earth.

"We believe that the Holy Mother of God, the new Eve, Mother of the Church, continues in Heaven to exercise her maternal role on behalf of the members of Christ" (Pope Paul VI, *Credo of the People of God*).

Our Response

In the Church's prayers to Mary, we "magnify" the Lord for the "great things" He did for His lowly servant and through her for all human beings (*CCC*, 2675).

By calling her our queen, the Church teaches us that we can put enormous faith in Mary's ability to intercede for us.

If Mary is my queen, she is queen of all aspects of my life; not just my religious life, but my social life, work life, home life—and private life—as well.

Pray for me, Mary, gate of Heaven,
that I will trust in the intercession of Mary in my great need.

The Litany of Loreto

V. Lord, have mercy.
R. Christ have mercy.
V. Lord have mercy.
Christ hear us.
R. Christ graciously hear us.
God the Father of Heaven,
have mercy on us.
God the Son, Redeemer of
the world, *have mercy on us.*
God the Holy Spirit,
have mercy on us.
Holy Trinity, one God,
have mercy on us.
Holy Mary, *pray for us.*
Holy Mother of God,
pray for us.
Holy Virgin of Virgins, [*etc.*]
Mother of Christ,
Mother of Divine Grace,
Mother most pure,
Mother most chaste,
Mother inviolate,
Mother undefiled,
Mother most amiable,
Mother most admirable,
Mother of good counsel,

Mother of our Creator,
Mother of our Savior,
Virgin most prudent,
Virgin most venerable,
Virgin most renowned,
Virgin most powerful,
Virgin most merciful,
Virgin most faithful,
Mirror of justice,
Seat of wisdom,
Cause of our joy,
Spiritual vessel,
Vessel of honor,
Singular vessel of devotion,
Mystical rose,
Tower of David,
Tower of ivory,
House of gold,
Ark of the covenant,
Gate of Heaven,
Morning star,
Health of the sick,
Refuge of sinners,
Comforter of the afflicted,
Help of Christians,
Queen of Angels,

Queen of Patriarchs,
Queen of Prophets,
Queen of Apostles,
Queen of Martyrs,
Queen of Confessors,
Queen of Virgins,
Queen of all Saints,
Queen conceived without original sin,
Queen assumed into Heaven,
Queen of the most holy Rosary,
Queen of families,
Queen of peace,
V. Lamb of God, Who takest away the sins of the world,
R. Spare us, O Lord.
V. Lamb of God, Who takest away the sins of the world,
R. Graciously hear us, O Lord.
V. Lamb of God, Who takest away the sins of the world,
Have mercy on us.
V. Pray for us, O holy Mother of God.
R. That we may be made worthy of the promises of Christ.

Let us pray. Grant, we beseech Thee, O Lord God, that we Thy servants may enjoy perpetual health of mind and body, and by the glorious intercession of blessed Mary, ever Virgin, may we be freed from present sorrow, and rejoice in eternal happiness. Through Christ our Lord. *R. Amen.*

Salve Regina
(Hail, Holy Queen)

Hail, holy Queen, Mother of mercy, our life, our sweetness and our hope. To thee do we cry, poor banished children of Eve. To thee to we send up our sighs, mourning and weeping in this valley of tears. Turn, then, most gracious advocate, thine eyes of mercy toward us, and after this, our exile, show unto us the blessed fruit of thy womb, Jesus. O clement, O loving, O sweet Virgin Mary.

V. Pray for us, O holy Mother of God.
R. That we may be made worthy of the promises of Christ.

A *plenary indulgence* is granted to the faithful who (under the ordinary conditions):

> Devoutly recite the Marian Rosary in a church or oratory, or in a family, a religious community, or an association of the faithful, and in general when several of the faithful gather for some honest purpose;

> Devoutly join in the recitation of the Rosary while it is being recited by the Supreme Pontiff and broadcast live by radio or television. In other circumstances, the indulgence will be *partial*.

According to the *Manual of Indulgences* (English translation copyright ©2006 Libreria Editrice Vaticana), the plenary indulgence is gained when only five decades of the Rosary are recited. However, the five decades must be recited without interruption.

More Devotional Books from Holy Heroes!

Order online at **www.HolyHeroes.com**

The Stations of the Cross (Via Crucis)
Bi-lingual Prayer Booklet

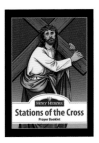

Two-in-one "flip" book with English on one side and Spanish on the other. The traditional 14 Stations of the Cross, including the Stabat Mater verse at every station and artwork to aid in meditation. The concluding prayer is the "Prayer before a Crucifix" of Saint Francis of Assisi. Includes an introduction and "How to pray the Stations of the Cross." Great for children to lead the Stations in a parish, classroom, or family setting. (64 pages: 32 for each language)

The Fatima Family Handbook
Heaven's Plan for Your Family

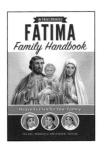

Learn Heaven's plan for your family as revealed through the miraculous visits to Francisco and Jacinta Marto and Lucia dos Santos in Fatima, Portugal, one-hundred years ago! Includes the prayers they were taught and their own explanations of what the apparitions taught them about the Faith and how to live it. See for yourself how Fatima can be considered "a mini-catechism," providing supernatural proof for so many truths of the Faith! (64 pages in full color)

Corporal and Spiritual Works of Mercy Book
How God's Love Transforms Your Heart!

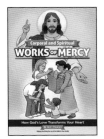

Teach your children all 14 Works of Mercy! This book is dedicated to Saints Mother Teresa and Faustina, so you'll also learn about Divine Mercy, Mercy in the Mass, what Jesus told Saint Faustina was His "Tribunal of Mercy," and much more! Charming artwork will engage children's minds and hearts. This is a companion book to our "Works of Mercy" card game! (48 pages, full-color, illustrated)

Best-Loved Catholic Prayers and Prayers of the Mass
Missalette and Prayers Flip-Book

The Prayer Flip-Book contains over two dozen traditional Catholic prayers and devotions, with explanations and background to take you from your Morning Offering to evening Examination of Conscience, with favorite Latin prayers, too.

The Missalette section contains prayers and responses according to the Third Edition of the Roman Missal. Mass postures in blue, other comments in red, and even some of the typical responses in Latin and Greek. Imprimatur and approved by the USCCB.

(48 pages in full color)

About the Author

Tom Hoopes is Writer in Residence and Vice President of College Relations at Benedictine College, where he is also an Adjunct Professor in the Journalism and Mass Communication Department. He has written regularly for the *National Catholic Register* and *Aleteia*, reaching a national and international audience. His work has also appeared in *Catholic Digest*, *Columbia* magazine, *Crisis* magazine and *First Things* online. His first book for Holy Heroes was *The Fatima Family Handbook: Heaven's Plan for Your Family*.

Tom is a graduate of the St. Ignatius Institute at the University of San Francisco and received his MBA from Benedictine College. He was editor of the *National Catholic Register* for ten years and *Faith & Family* magazine for five. He lives in Atchison, Kansas, with his wife, April, and those of his nine children who have not already left for college and adulthood.